The Smart Millennial's Guide to Money Management and Wealth Building

By Jules Carlysle

Table of Contents

Introduction

Welcome to a journey that could very well reshape your financial future. In the pages that follow, you will discover the secrets and strategies that can unlock the potential of your money, empowering you to build wealth and secure your financial freedom. This is not just a book; it's a roadmap to a more prosperous future. Whether you are fresh out of college, embarking on your first job, or simply a young adult eager to take control of your financial destiny, the knowledge you're about to gain is invaluable.

Let's start with a fundamental truth: time is your greatest ally in the realm of wealth building. The power of compounding interest, often hailed as the eighth wonder of the world, is at its most potent when you start early. Imagine a snowball rolling down a hill, gathering more snow and momentum as it goes – that's your wealth growing over time. Each day that passes is an opportunity for your money to grow, to build upon itself, creating wealth that can surpass your wildest expectations. The earlier you start, the less you have to invest to achieve the same goal. This is the magic of compound interest and the undeniable value of time.

However, harnessing this power requires more than just knowledge; it demands the right mindset. Successful money management and wealth building are not just about understanding finances; they are about cultivating a mindset that prioritizes saving, investing, and making informed financial decisions. It's about looking at money not just as a means to spend, but as a tool to create a future you desire. This mindset isn't inborn; it's developed through discipline, education, and a willingness to learn from both successes and failures.

In embarking on this financial adventure, you may encounter several myths about wealth building that can deter or mislead young adults. These include misconceptions like "investing is only for the rich," or "it's too early to think about retirement." These myths are not just false; they are dangerous, as they can lead to missed opportunities and a lack of preparation for the future. This book aims to dispel these myths, arming you with the facts and strategies you need to make informed decisions about your money.

Remember, the journey to financial freedom is a marathon, not a sprint. It's about making consistent, smart choices over time, and staying informed and adaptable as your financial needs and the world around you evolve. As you turn these pages, keep an open mind, and be ready to challenge your preconceptions about money. With each chapter, you're not just reading; you're investing in yourself and your future.

So, let's begin this exciting journey together. Your future self will thank you for the wisdom and insights you're about to gain.

10

Chapter 1

The Fundamentals of Financial Freedom

Financial freedom - it's a phrase often tossed around in conversations about wealth and success. But what does it truly mean, especially for you as a young adult? Simply put, financial freedom is the state of having sufficient personal wealth to live without having to work actively for basic necessities. It means your assets generate income that exceeds your expenses. Achieving this might sound like a lofty goal, especially when you're just starting, but it's far from unattainable. This chapter explores what financial freedom means, breaks down key financial terms, and guides you on setting effective financial goals.

1. Defining Financial Freedom: A Reality, Not Just a Dream

Imagine waking up each morning with a clear choice of how to spend your day because you are not weighed down by financial obligations. That's the essence of financial freedom. It's not about living an extravagant lifestyle; it's about having control over your time and choices.

Take Sarah, for example. She started saving a portion of her income from her first job at 22. By living modestly and investing wisely, Sarah was able to achieve financial independence by 40. She now spends her time traveling, pursuing hobbies, and volunteering, not out of necessity but because she chooses to.

2. Key Financial Terms Every Young Adult Should Know

Understanding financial terminology is crucial. It's like learning a new language that will help you navigate your wealth-building journey.

- **Assets and Liabilities:** Simply put, assets put money in your pocket (like investments or rental properties), while liabilities take money out (like loans or debts).
- **Net Worth:** This is what you own minus what you owe. It's a critical measure of your financial health.
- **Investments:** These are vehicles like stocks, bonds, real estate, or mutual funds where you put your money, expecting it to grow over time.
- **Compound Interest:** This is interest calculated on the initial principal, which also

includes all of the accumulated interest from previous periods on a deposit or loan.

Tom and Compound Interest Consider Tom, who started investing a small amount in a mutual fund at 25. Thanks to compound interest, by the time he was 50, his initial investment had grown exponentially, significantly outpacing what he could have saved by simply putting money in a savings account.

3. Setting Financial Goals and Creating a Vision for the Future

Setting clear financial goals is like having a roadmap for your journey. Whether it's saving for a down payment on a house, funding a dream vacation, or preparing for retirement, your goals should be specific, measurable, achievable, relevant, and time-bound (SMART).

Emily's Vision Board Emily, at 23, created a vision board with her financial goals, including buying a car, traveling to Europe, and owning a home before 30. This visual representation kept her focused and motivated. By 29, she had ticked off each goal, thanks to her disciplined saving and investing strategy.

Conclusion

Financial freedom is not a myth reserved for the select few; it's a realistic goal that you can achieve with the right knowledge and mindset. Understanding key financial concepts and setting clear goals are your first steps on this journey. In the following chapters, we'll dive deeper into strategies and tools that will help you build and maintain your wealth. Remember, every big journey starts with small, determined steps. Your path to financial freedom begins now.

Chapter 2
Money Management Mastery

Mastering money management is a vital skill for any young adult aspiring towards financial independence. This chapter will guide you through the basics of budgeting, building and maintaining excellent credit, and developing smart spending habits. Each section is reinforced with anecdotes, providing real-world examples of these principles in action.

1. Budgeting Basics for the Young Adult
Budgeting isn't about restricting yourself—it's about understanding and controlling where your money goes. Start by tracking your income and expenses. Categorize your expenses into 'needs' (like rent and groceries) and 'wants' (like eating out and entertainment). Use tools like budgeting apps or spreadsheets to make this process easier.

Jake's Spreadsheet Success Jake, a recent college graduate, began tracking his expenses in a simple spreadsheet. He set limits for different categories and adjusted his spending accordingly. This simple act of tracking helped Jake save enough for a down payment on his first car within a year.

Steps to Create a Budget:
- **List Your Income Sources:** Include your salary, any side hustles, or passive income.
- **Track Your Expenses:** Record every purchase or payment.
- **Set Spending Limits:** Base them on your expense tracking and financial goals.
- **Review and Adjust Monthly:** As your income or expenses change, so should your budget.

2. Building and Maintaining Excellent Credit
Your credit score is a crucial component of your financial health. It affects your ability to borrow money, the interest rates you get, and can even influence job opportunities and what apartment you can rent.

Key Steps to Building Credit:

- **Get a Credit Card:** Use it for small, regular purchases and pay it off in full each month.
- **Pay Bills On Time:** Set reminders or automate payments.

- **Keep Credit Utilization Low:** Try not to use more than 30% of your available credit.
- **Monitor Your Credit Report:** Check for inaccuracies and learn from your credit habits.

Lisa's Credit Turnaround Lisa incurred some credit card debt in college, negatively impacting her credit score. By creating a debt payment plan and following these steps, she gradually rebuilt her credit, allowing her to secure a favorable loan for her first home.

3. Smart Spending Habits and Avoiding Financial Pitfalls

Developing smart spending habits means making informed and intentional choices with your money. It's about aligning your spending with your values and long-term goals.

Omar's Smart Spending Shift Omar loved eating out frequently, but when he calculated how much he was spending per month, he was shocked. By reducing dining out to special occasions and cooking more at home, he was able to start an investment fund.

Avoiding Common Financial Pitfalls:

- **Avoid Impulse Purchases:** Wait 24 hours before making significant purchases.
- **Be Wary of "Lifestyle Creep":** As your income increases, so can unnecessary spending.
- **Steer Clear of High-Interest Debt:** Avoid payday loans and high-interest credit cards.

Conclusion

Effective money management is the cornerstone of building wealth. By mastering budgeting, establishing good credit, and developing smart spending habits, you are laying a solid foundation for your financial future. Remember, these habits don't form overnight, but with persistence and discipline, they will become second nature. As we move to the next chapter, keep in mind that every smart financial decision you make brings you one step closer to your goals.

Chapter 3
Compound Interest – Your Best Friend in Wealth Building

Understanding and harnessing the power of compound interest is crucial in your wealth-building journey. Often referred to as the eighth wonder of the world, compound interest can transform modest savings into substantial wealth over time. This chapter delves into the mechanics of compound interest, how you can leverage it in your savings and investments, and the tools and accounts that maximize its benefits, all illustrated with practical examples and anecdotes.

1. The Power of Compound Interest Explained
Compound interest is interest calculated on the initial principal of a deposit or loan, which also includes all of the accumulated interest from previous periods. In simpler terms, it's earning interest on interest. Over time, this results in exponentially increasing growth of your investment.

The Tale of Two Savers Consider two friends, Alex and Jordan. At age 25, Alex starts saving $200 a *month in an account that earns 5% annual compound interest. Jordan starts doing the same at age 35. By the time they both reach 60, Alex has contributed $84,000 while Jordan has contributed $60,000. However, due to the power of compounding, Alex has over $170,000 more in savings than Jordan, despite only contributing $24,000 more.*

2. Leveraging Compound Interest in Savings and Investments

To make the most of compound interest, start saving and investing as early as possible. The longer your money is invested, the more time it has to grow.

Strategies to Leverage Compound Interest:

- **Start Early:** Even small amounts saved early can outgrow larger amounts saved at a later stage.
- **Regular Contributions:** Consistently adding to your savings or investment accounts increases the base amount on which interest is compounded.
- **Reinvest Dividends and Interest:** Allow your earnings to be reinvested to benefit from compound growth.

Mia's Investment Journey Mia, a graphic designer, began investing a small portion of her income in a diversified stock portfolio at the age of 30. She chose investments that paid dividends, which she automatically reinvested. Over the years, this strategy allowed her portfolio to grow significantly more than if she had taken the dividends as cash.

3. Tools and Accounts to Maximize Compound Interest Benefits

Several financial products and accounts are designed to maximize the benefits of compound interest.

Key Tools and Accounts:

- **High-Interest Savings Accounts:** These accounts offer higher interest rates than regular savings accounts, leading to better compounding effects.
- **Retirement Accounts (such as 401(k)s Tax-Free Savings Accounts and IRAs):** These accounts benefit from tax advantages, allowing your investments to grow tax-free or tax-deferred.
- **Certificates of Deposit (CDs):** CDs often offer higher interest rates in exchange for leaving your money untouched for a set period.

- **Mutual Funds and ETFs:** These investment vehicles allow you to diversify your portfolio and benefit from compound interest across various assets.

Kevin's Roth IRA Kevin started contributing to a Roth IRA in his early twenties. The Roth IRA allowed his investments to grow tax-free, and he didn't have to pay taxes on withdrawals during retirement. This tax advantage, combined with the compound interest earned over decades, significantly increased his retirement funds.

Conclusion

Compound interest can be a powerful ally in wealth building, but it requires time, discipline, and consistency. By starting early, reinvesting earnings, and choosing the right financial tools and accounts, you can harness the full potential of compound interest. Remember, the key to benefiting from compound interest is patience and long-term commitment. As we progress to the next chapters, keep in mind that the decisions you make today about your finances have the potential to shape your financial landscape for years to come.

Chapter 4
Entering the Stock Market

For many young adults, the stock market represents both an opportunity and a challenge. It's a platform where fortunes can be made and, unfortunately, lost. This chapter aims to demystify stock market investing, explaining stocks, bonds, and mutual funds, and discussing the risks and rewards. It also provides strategies for long-term investing, such as index funds and ETFs, supplemented with real-life anecdotes.

1. Understanding Stocks, Bonds, and Mutual Funds

Stocks: When you buy stocks, you're purchasing a small part of a company. As the company's value grows, so does the value of your stock. Conversely, if the company does poorly, your stock's value may decrease.

Bonds: Bonds are essentially loans you give to a company or government, in exchange for periodic interest payments. At the end of the bond term, the initial investment is returned. They are generally considered safer than stocks but offer lower returns.

Mutual Funds: These are investment vehicles that pool money from many investors to buy a diversified portfolio of stocks, bonds, or other securities. They are managed by professional fund managers.

Rachel's Diverse Portfolio Rachel started investing with a mix of stocks and bonds in her early twenties. While her stocks saw significant fluctuations, her bonds provided a steady, though smaller, return. This diversification helped balance her portfolio during market ups and downs.

2. Risks and Rewards of Stock Market Investing
Investing in the stock market involves risk, but with greater risk can come greater reward. The key is to understand your risk tolerance and invest accordingly.

- **Market Volatility:** The stock market can be unpredictable, with prices fluctuating due to various factors.
- **Potential High Returns:** Historically, the stock market has provided higher returns than savings accounts or bonds over the long term.
- **Risk of Loss:** There's always a chance you could lose your entire investment, especially if you're investing in individual stocks.

Sam's Tech Stock Experience Sam invested heavily in a single tech stock, drawn by its rapid growth. Unfortunately, the stock plummeted due to unexpected industry changes, leading to significant losses. This experience taught Sam the importance of not putting all his eggs in one basket.

3. Strategies for Long-Term Investing

For long-term wealth building, strategies such as investing in index funds and ETFs (Exchange-Traded Funds) are often recommended.

- **Index Funds:** These funds track a specific market index, like the S&P 500. They offer diversification and typically have lower fees.
- **ETFs:** Similar to index funds, ETFs are traded like individual stocks and offer a way to invest in a broad market segment or industry.

Anita's Index Fund Success Anita started investing in an S&P 500 index fund through a monthly automatic investment plan. Over two decades, despite market fluctuations, her initial investments grew significantly, outpacing inflation and savings account interest rates.

4. Building a Diverse Portfolio

Diversification is key in stock market investing. It involves spreading your investments across different types of assets (stocks, bonds, real estate, etc.), industries, and geographic locations to reduce risk. *David's Global Investment David diversified his portfolio by investing in international ETFs, spreading his risk beyond the U.S. market. This strategy paid off when the U.S. market was sluggish, but international markets were performing well.*

Conclusion

Entering the stock market is an exciting step in your financial journey. While it comes with risks, informed and strategic investing, particularly with a focus on long-term gains and diversification, can be immensely rewarding. Remember, investing is not a get-rich-quick scheme but a way to build wealth over time. In the next chapter, we will explore the exciting world of real estate investing, another key component in your wealth-building strategy.

Chapter 5

Real Estate as a Wealth Tool

Real estate investment has long been hailed as a reliable means to build wealth. For young adults, it presents a unique set of opportunities and challenges. This chapter will explore the basics of real estate investing, the different avenues available for young investors, and the pros and cons of diving into the real estate market.

1. Basics of Real Estate Investing

Real estate investing involves purchasing property to hold long term as it appreciates, to generate rental income or to fix up and resell at a higher value. It's different from owning a primary residence, as the focus is on income generation and investment growth.

- **Understanding the Market:** Research local market trends, property values, and rental rates.
- **Financing:** Know your options for mortgages and loans, and understand the implications of interest rates and loan terms.

- **Due Diligence:** Evaluate the condition of the property, potential repair costs, and legal considerations like zoning and property taxes.

2. Different Ways to Invest in Real Estate at a Young Age

Real estate investment isn't limited to buying physical properties. There are several accessible options for young adults:

- **Real Estate Investment Trusts (REITs):** REITs are companies that own or finance income-generating real estate. By investing in a REIT, you can earn dividends without dealing with the complexities of owning physical property.
- **Real Estate Crowdfunding:** Platforms allow individuals to invest small amounts of money in real estate projects, offering a way to diversify investments.
- **Owning and Renting Property:** If financially feasible, purchasing property to rent out can provide a steady stream of income and capital appreciation.

Maria's REIT Journey Maria, interested in real estate but lacking substantial capital, started investing in REITs through her online brokerage account. This allowed her to tap into the real estate market without the need for a large upfront investment.

3. Pros and Cons of Real Estate Investment
Like any investment, real estate has its upsides and downsides:

- **Pros:**
    - **Potential for Steady Income:** Rental properties can provide a regular income stream.
    - **Capital Appreciation:** Over time, real estate typically appreciates in value.
    - **Tax Advantages:** Real estate investors often benefit from deductions and depreciation.

- **Cons:**
    - **Capital Intensive:** Purchasing property requires a significant upfront investment.
    - **Market Risks:** Real estate markets can fluctuate, and properties can lose value.
    - **Management Challenges:** Owning and managing rental properties requires time and effort.

Dylan's Rental Property Dylan invested in a small rental property. While he enjoyed a steady rental income, he also faced challenges like maintenance issues and managing tenant relationships. His experience highlighted both the income potential and the hands-on involvement required in property management.

Conclusion

Real estate investment can be a valuable tool in building wealth, but it requires careful consideration and planning. Whether through physical property, REITs, or crowdfunding, real estate offers diverse opportunities for young investors. As with all investments, it's important to assess your financial situation, do thorough research, and consider seeking advice from financial experts. In the next chapter, we'll shift our focus to a unique and often overlooked aspect of wealth building: investing in collectibles and alternative assets.

Chapter 6
Alternative Investments:
Collectibles and More

While traditional investments like stocks and real estate form the backbone of most wealth-building strategies, alternative investments, particularly in collectibles such as art, coins, trading cards, and even designer goods, can offer not only financial rewards but also personal enjoyment. This chapter will guide you through the intriguing world of investing in collectibles, understanding their value and market trends, and the importance of risk management.

1. An Introduction to Investing in Collectibles
Collectibles are unique items that can appreciate in value over time due to their rarity, demand, historical significance, or cultural value.

Examples include:

- **Art:** Original paintings, sculptures, and limited-edition prints.

- **Coins and Currency:** Rare, historical, or limited-mint coins and bills.
- **Trading Cards:** Sports cards, game cards (like Magic: The Gathering), and others.
- **Designer Goods:** High-end designer handbags, watches, and fashion accessories.
- **Toys:**
- **Antiques:**

Each category has its own nuances, market, and community of enthusiasts.

2. Understanding Value, Rarity, and Market Trends

The value of a collectible is influenced by several factors:

- **Rarity and Condition:** Generally, the rarer and better the condition, the more valuable the item.
- **Provenance and Authenticity:** The history and authenticity of an item can greatly impact its value.
- **Market Demand:** Trends in collector interest can drive prices up or down.

Market Research is Key: Successful investing in collectibles involves continuous learning and staying abreast of market trends. Subscribing to specialized magazines, joining collector groups, and attending auctions can provide valuable insights.

3. Risk Management and Avoiding Fads
Investing in collectibles comes with unique risks, and it's vital to approach this market with caution:

- **Illiquid Market:** Unlike stocks or bonds, selling collectibles can take time, and finding buyers may not always be easy.
- **Market Volatility:** The value of collectibles can be highly volatile, influenced by changing trends and collector interest.
- **Fads:** Beware of investing in items that are momentarily popular but may not hold long-term value.

Case Study: The Beanie Baby Craze In the late 1990s, Beanie Babies became a national craze, with some items fetching thousands of dollars. However, when the fad faded, many investors were left with collections worth a fraction of their peak value, illustrating the risks of following short-term trends.

Conclusion
Investing in collectibles can be a fulfilling and potentially profitable endeavor, but it requires a passion for the items, an understanding of the

market, and a cautious approach to risk. In the next chapter, we will explore the final pillar of wealth building for young adults: mastering the art of negotiation and communication in financial dealings.

Chapter 7
Building Wealth Through Entrepreneurship

Entrepreneurship offers a dynamic path to wealth building, allowing young adults to turn their passions into profitable ventures. This chapter delves into the process of starting a business or side hustle, the basics of entrepreneurship, and essential financial management practices, supplemented with real-world examples.

1. Turning Passions into Profit
The first step in entrepreneurship is often identifying a passion or a market need and transforming it into a viable business idea.

- **Identify Your Niche:** Look for a market need that aligns with your interests or skills.
- **Market Research:** Understand your target audience and what makes your offering unique.
- **Validation:** Test your idea through small-scale trials or prototypes to gauge interest.

Liam's Eco-Friendly Apparel Brand Liam, passionate about environmental sustainability, launched a line of eco-friendly clothing. By targeting a specific niche, he was able to build a brand that resonated with environmentally conscious consumers.

2. Basics of Starting a Business or Side Hustle

Starting a business or a side hustle requires strategic planning and a grasp of the basics:

- **Business Plan:** Develop a clear plan outlining your business model, marketing strategy, and financial projections.
- **Legal Structure:** Decide on a business structure (e.g., sole proprietorship, LLC) that fits your needs and protects you legally.
- **Building a Brand:** Focus on creating a strong brand identity and online presence.

Zoe's Freelance Graphic Design Business Zoe started as a freelance graphic designer during college. By creating a professional website and portfolio, and listing her services on Apps like Fiverr, she attracted clients and gradually built a thriving business.

3. Financial Management for the Young Entrepreneur

Effective financial management is critical for the success and growth of any entrepreneurial venture:

- **Budgeting and Expenses:** Keep track of all business expenses and create a budget to manage cash flow.
- **Funding Your Business:** Explore funding options, from bootstrapping to seeking angel investors or loans.
- **Accounting and Taxes:** Maintain accurate records for all transactions and understand the tax implications of your business activities.

Carlos's Food Truck Venture Carlos launched a food truck business. He meticulously recorded all expenses and income, used budgeting to control costs, and kept aside a portion of his earnings for taxes. His attention to financial detail helped him avoid problems with cash flow and the IRS.

Conclusion

Entrepreneurship is not just about starting a business; it's about cultivating a mindset of innovation, risk-taking, and financial savvy. Whether it's turning a hobby into a side hustle or launching a full-scale start-up, the journey of entrepreneurship can be a rewarding path to building wealth. In our final chapter, we will explore the importance of networking, mentorship, and continuous learning in the journey of wealth building.

Chapter 8
Tech-Savvy Investing

In the digital age, technology plays a crucial role in personal finance and investing. This chapter focuses on leveraging technology for smarter budgeting and investing, understanding the role of robo-advisors, and introducing the concepts of cryptocurrency and blockchain technology. These tools and innovations can empower young adults to make more informed and efficient financial decisions.

1. Using Technology for Budgeting and Investing
The proliferation of apps and platforms has made managing finances more accessible and efficient than ever before.

- **Budgeting Apps:** Tools like Mint, YNAB (You Need A Budget), and PocketGuard help track spending, set budgets, and monitor savings goals.
- **Investment Platforms:** Apps such as WealthSimple, Robinhood, Acorns, and Betterment offer easy access to stock markets, ETFs, and other investment options with user-friendly interfaces.

Aisha's Budgeting Success Aisha, a recent college graduate, used a budgeting app to track her expenses and savings. The app's insights helped her identify unnecessary expenditures and increase her monthly savings.

2. The Role of Robo-Advisors
Robo-advisors have become a popular tool for automated, algorithm-driven financial planning services with little to no human supervision.

- **How They Work:** Robo-advisors collect information from clients about their financial situation and future goals through an online survey, then use the data to offer advice and/or automatically invest client assets.
- **Benefits:** They are generally low-cost, accessible, and provide a passive investing approach suitable for those starting in investment.

3. An Introduction to Cryptocurrency and Blockchain Technology
Cryptocurrency and blockchain are at the forefront of financial technology innovation. They are also unregulated, uninsured and fraught with potential dangers. Never EVER invest money that you can't afford to lose.

- **Cryptocurrency Basics:** Digital or virtual currencies that use cryptography for security. They are typically decentralized and based on blockchain technology.
- **Blockchain Explained:** A distributed ledger or database that is shared among the nodes of a computer network. It stores information electronically in digital format and is known for its security and transparency.
- **Investing in Cryptocurrency:** While potentially lucrative, cryptocurrency investments carry high risks and volatility. It's important to research thoroughly and invest cautiously.

Nadia's Dive into Cryptocurrency Nadia, intrigued by digital currencies, started small by investing a portion of her savings in a well-known cryptocurrency. She used a reputed exchange and kept herself updated on market trends and risks associated with crypto investments.

Conclusion

Technology has undoubtedly simplified many aspects of personal finance and investing. By utilizing these tech tools wisely, young adults can enhance their financial literacy, streamline their investing processes, and explore new investment frontiers like cryptocurrencies. However, it's essential to approach these tools with a blend of enthusiasm and caution, keeping in mind the importance of research and risk management. In the next chapter, we will wrap up our journey with final thoughts and key takeaways for young adults embarking on their wealth-building journey.

Chapter 9
Navigating Taxes and Income

Taxes play a significant role in personal finance and investment strategies. For young adults, understanding taxation and its impact on income and investments is crucial for effective wealth building. This chapter will provide a comprehensive guide on how taxation affects investments, the essentials of filing taxes as a young investor, and strategies to optimize tax savings.

1. **Understanding Taxation and Its Effects on Investments**
    Navigating the world of taxes can be challenging, but it's a vital skill for managing and growing wealth.

    *   **Types of Taxes on Investments:** Learn about capital gains taxes, dividend taxes, and taxes on interest income. Understand how these taxes vary based on investment types and holding periods.

    *   **Tax-Advantaged Accounts:** Explore investment options like Roth IRAs,

Traditional IRAs, and 401(k)s, which offer various tax benefits and can significantly impact your long-term savings.

Maya's Investment Tax Planning Maya, an avid investor, learned to align her investment strategy with tax planning. She utilized Roth IRA for her long-term investments to benefit from tax-free growth and withdrawals after retirement.

2. How to File Taxes as a Young Investor
Filing taxes can be daunting, especially when you have multiple income streams or investments.

- **Document Organization:** Keep track of all necessary documents such as W-2s, 1099s, and records of investments.
- **Understanding Tax Forms:** Get familiar with different tax forms and which ones apply to your financial situation.
- **Using Tax Software or Professional Help:** Consider using reliable tax software or consulting with a tax professional, especially if you have complex investment portfolios.
-

Alex's First Time Filing Taxes Alex, a recent graduate with his first full-time job and some stock investments, used an online tax software program. It guided him through the process, ensuring he correctly reported his income and investment gains.

3. Tips for Optimizing Tax Savings
Smart tax strategies can lead to substantial savings over time.

- **Maximizing Deductions and Credits:** Understand what deductions and credits you are eligible for, such as education credits or deductions for retirement account contributions.
- **Harvesting Tax Losses:** Learn about tax-loss harvesting, a strategy that involves selling investments at a loss to offset capital gains tax liabilities.
- **Strategic Investment Decisions:** Consider the tax implications of your investment choices, like investing in tax-exempt municipal bonds or timing the sale of assets.

Priya's Tax-Optimized Investments Priya utilized tax-loss harvesting to offset some of the capital gains she had realized in a particularly profitable investment year, effectively reducing her tax liability.

Conclusion

A solid understanding of how taxation intersects with income and investments is crucial for financial success. By being informed and strategic about taxes, young investors can make more educated decisions, leading to better financial outcomes. The next chapter will conclude our journey, offering a recap of the essential principles of wealth building and providing a roadmap for continuous financial growth and education.

Chapter 10
Risk Management and Insurance

Effective wealth building isn't just about earning and investing money; it also involves protecting the wealth you accumulate. This chapter discusses the critical role of insurance in safeguarding your financial future, outlines the types of insurance young adults should consider, and guides on evaluating insurance needs.

1. The Role of Insurance in Protecting Your Wealth
Insurance is a key tool in risk management, providing financial protection against unforeseen events that can have a significant impact on your finances.

- **Understanding Risk Exposure:** Learn how different types of risks can affect your financial health.
- **Insurance as a Safety Net:** Understand how insurance policies work as a safety net, helping you manage financial risks without depleting your savings or investments.

Sarah's Car Accident Sarah's decision to have comprehensive auto insurance proved invaluable when she was involved in a car accident. Her policy covered the majority of the repair costs, sparing her significant financial strain.

2. Types of Insurance Young Adults Should Consider
Various types of insurance cater to different aspects of risk management.

- **Health Insurance:** Essential for covering medical expenses, which can be financially devastating without coverage.
- **Life Insurance:** Important, especially if you have dependents or significant debt, to provide financial security to your beneficiaries.
- **Renters or Homeowners Insurance:** Protects your property and possessions from theft or damage.
- **Auto Insurance:** A legal requirement in many places, it covers damages from accidents.
- **Disability Insurance:** Provides income if you're unable to work due to illness or injury.

Kevin's Health Scare When Kevin faced an unexpected health issue requiring surgery, his health insurance covered most of the hefty medical bills, allowing him to focus on recovery without financial distress.

3. How to Evaluate Insurance Needs
Determining the right type and amount of insurance requires careful consideration of your specific circumstances.

- **Assessing Your Situation:** Consider factors like age, health, lifestyle, dependents, and assets.
- **Coverage Levels:** Understand the coverage level you need to protect yourself adequately without overpaying for unnecessary coverage.
- **Comparing Policies:** Look at various policies to find the best coverage at a reasonable price.

Rita's Insurance Review Rita evaluated her insurance needs upon buying a new house. She increased her life insurance coverage to ensure her mortgage was covered and shopped around for the best homeowners' insurance rates, balancing coverage and cost.

Conclusion

Insurance is an essential component of a comprehensive wealth-building strategy, offering protection against various risks that can erode financial stability. By carefully assessing needs and choosing appropriate insurance products, young adults can safeguard their hard-earned wealth against life's uncertainties. In our final chapter, we will wrap up the key themes of the book and offer a forward-looking perspective on maintaining and growing wealth through various life stages.

Chapter 11
Financial Planning for Major Life Events

Major life events, whether anticipated or unexpected, can have a substantial impact on your financial landscape. This chapter focuses on financial planning strategies for significant milestones such as higher education, travel, home buying, marriage, and the importance of an emergency fund for unforeseen events.

1. Planning and Saving for Higher Education, Travel, or Buying a Home
Strategic financial planning is key when preparing for substantial expenses like education, travel, or home ownership.

- **Higher Education:** Explore saving options like 529 plans or education savings accounts. Consider scholarships, grants, and student loans, understanding their long-term impact.
- **Travel:** Budgeting for travel involves setting aside money regularly. Learn about travel rewards programs and budget travel tips.

- **Home Buying:** Understand the process of saving for a down payment, the importance of a good credit score, and the various mortgage options available.

Jason's Education Fund Jason started a 529 plan early for his daughter's education, allowing his contributions to grow tax-free, significantly reducing the financial burden when she started college.

2. Financial Considerations for Marriage and Partnerships
Combining finances with a partner requires careful planning and open communication.

- **Budgeting Together:** Discuss financial goals, debts, and income. Create a joint budget that works for both partners.
- **Joint vs. Separate Accounts:** Weigh the pros and cons of having joint bank accounts, separate accounts, or a combination.
- **Planning for the Future:** Discuss long-term goals like retirement planning, investments, and purchasing property together.

Nina and Omar's Financial Dialogue Nina and Omar held regular financial meetings to discuss their budgets, goals, and investments, ensuring they were aligned in their financial journey as a couple.

3. Preparing for Unforeseen Events with an Emergency Fund

An emergency fund is a financial safety net designed to cover unexpected expenses or financial emergencies.

- **Importance of an Emergency Fund:** Understand how an emergency fund can protect you from debt and financial stress in the case of unforeseen events like job loss or medical emergencies.
- **How Much to Save:** General guidelines suggest saving three to six months' worth of living expenses.
- **Building the Fund:** Learn strategies to gradually build an emergency fund, such as automating savings or allocating a portion of bonuses or tax refunds.

Layla's Lifesaver Fund When Layla unexpectedly lost her job, her emergency fund covered her living expenses for five months, giving her the peace of mind and time necessary to find a new position without financial desperation.

Conclusion

Planning for major life events is a critical aspect of financial management. By anticipating and saving for these milestones, you can enjoy life's journey without compromising your financial stability. Each of these events presents unique challenges and opportunities, and being financially prepared ensures that you can embrace them with confidence and security. As we conclude this book, remember that financial planning is a dynamic process that evolves with your life stages, and continuous learning and adaptation are key to successful wealth building.

Chapter 12
Socially Responsible and Ethical Investing

In recent years, there's been a significant shift towards investing not just for financial return but also for positive social and environmental impact. This chapter explores the concept of socially responsible and ethical investing, helping young adults align their investment choices with their personal values and societal concerns.

1. Aligning Your Investments with Your Values
Making investment decisions that reflect personal ethics and values is an integral part of socially responsible investing.

- **Identifying Your Values:** Begin by identifying what matters most to you – be it environmental sustainability, social justice, or corporate ethics.
- **Aligning Investments:** Learn how to align these values with your investment choices. This might mean investing in companies that

prioritize renewable energy, fair labor practices, or ethical governance.

Emma's Ethical Portfolio Emma, passionate about environmental conservation, chose to invest in a portfolio that exclusively contained companies with strong records in sustainability and renewable energy practices.

2. Understanding ESG (Environmental, Social, and Governance) Investing

ESG investing considers a company's practices in environmental stewardship, social responsibility, and governance.

- **Environmental Factors:** Look at how companies perform as stewards of the natural environment.
- **Social Factors:** Assess how a company manages relationships with employees, suppliers, customers, and communities.
- **Governance Factors:** Evaluate a company's leadership, executive pay, audits, internal controls, and shareholder rights.

Raj's ESG Approach Raj carefully selected his investments based on ESG ratings, focusing on companies that not only performed well financially but also had strong records in ethical governance and social responsibility.

3. How to Assess the Social Impact of Your Investment Choices

Assessing the social impact of investments involves looking beyond financial metrics to gauge a company's broader societal influence.

- **Researching Companies and Funds:** Utilize resources and tools to research and assess the ESG performance of companies and funds.
- **Balancing Impact and Returns:** Understand how to balance the social and environmental impact with the financial returns of your investments.
- **Avoiding 'Greenwashing':** Be aware of 'greenwashing', where companies overstate their positive environmental impact. Learn how to spot and avoid such misleading claims.
-

Aisha's Vigilant Selection Aisha learned to look deeply into companies' actual practices versus their public statements, avoiding those whose claims of social responsibility didn't hold up under scrutiny.

Conclusion

Socially responsible and ethical investing is a powerful way for young adults to make a positive impact on the world, aligning their investment strategies with their values and ethical beliefs. By carefully selecting investments based on ESG criteria, investors can contribute to positive change while also seeking financial returns. As young investors become more aware of the broader impact of their investment choices, they have the opportunity to shape a more ethical and sustainable future. Remember, investing isn't just about the return on investment; it's also about making a positive difference in the world.

Chapter 13
Building Your Wealth Network

Building wealth is not just about managing money and investments; it's also about surrounding yourself with a network of knowledgeable, experienced individuals who can offer guidance, support, and opportunities. This chapter delves into the importance of mentorship, the benefits of joining investment clubs and online communities, and the value of networking with successful investors.

1. The Importance of Mentorship and Financial Education

Having a mentor or participating in financial education programs can significantly enhance your understanding of wealth building.

- **Seeking Mentorship:** Understand the value of finding a mentor who has successfully navigated the financial landscape. A mentor

can offer personalized advice, share their experiences, and provide valuable insights.
- **Financial Education Programs:** Explore various programs and workshops that offer financial education. These can range from local community classes to online courses and seminars.

Maya's Mentorship Journey Maya credits her financial success to her mentor, a seasoned investor who guided her through her early investment decisions, helping her avoid common pitfalls and develop a robust investment strategy.

2. Joining Investment Clubs and Online Communities

Investment clubs and online communities provide platforms to learn, share experiences, and get support from peers.

- **Benefits of Investment Clubs:** Learn how joining an investment club can offer collaborative learning experiences, investment pooling opportunities, and a sense of community.
- **Online Financial Communities:** Explore online forums, YouTube, Reddit, social media groups, and financial blogs where young

investors share experiences, advice, and resources.

Liam's Learning Curve Liam joined an online investment community where he participated in discussions, shared his investment ideas, and received feedback, which broadened his understanding and confidence in making investment decisions.

3. Networking and Learning from Successful Investors

Interacting with successful investors can offer invaluable insights into effective wealth-building strategies.

- **Networking Opportunities:** Identify networking opportunities such as financial conferences, seminars, and local business events where you can meet and learn from experienced investors.
- **Learning from Others' Experiences:** Understand how learning from others' successes and failures can provide practical lessons in wealth building.

Zoe's Networking Success Zoe attended a local investment seminar where she connected with a successful real estate investor. This connection not only expanded her knowledge but also opened doors to new investment opportunities.

Conclusion

Building a wealth network is a critical step in your journey towards financial success. By seeking mentorship, joining investment clubs, participating in online communities, and networking with experienced investors, you can gain a wealth of knowledge, resources, and support. This network not only enriches your understanding of wealth building but also provides a platform for shared experiences and collaborative growth. Remember, the journey to financial freedom is not a solitary one – it's a path best navigated with the support and wisdom of a community.

Glossary

Here's a glossary of key investment terms and financial jargon to help you navigate the complex world of personal finance and investing. Understanding these terms is essential for effective money management and making informed investment decisions.

1. **Asset:** Anything of value that you own which can provide future economic benefits. Assets include cash, investments, property, etc.
2. **Bond:** A fixed-income instrument representing a loan made by an investor to a borrower. Bonds are used by companies, municipalities, states, and governments to finance projects and operations.
3. **Budget:** A financial plan that outlines expected income and expenditures over a period, helping manage your money effectively.
4. **Compound Interest:** Interest calculated on the initial principal and also on the accumulated interest of previous periods.
5. **Credit Score:** A number between 300-850 that depicts a consumer's creditworthiness.

The higher the score, the better a borrower looks to potential lenders.

6. **Diversification:** A risk management strategy that mixes a wide variety of investments within a portfolio.
7. **Dividend:** A distribution of a portion of a company's earnings to its shareholders.
8. **ETF (Exchange-Traded Fund):** A type of security that tracks an index, sector, commodity, or other assets, but can be bought and sold on a stock exchange the same as a regular stock.
9. **Index Fund:** A type of mutual fund with a portfolio constructed to match or track the components of a financial market index.
10. **Liquidity:** The ease with which an asset, or security, can be converted into ready cash without affecting its market price.
11. **Mutual Fund:** An investment vehicle made up of a pool of funds collected from many investors to invest in securities like stocks, bonds, money market instruments, and other assets.
12. **Portfolio:** A range of investments held by an individual or institution.
13. **REIT (Real Estate Investment Trust):** A company that owns, operates, or finances income-generating real estate. Modeled after mutual funds, REITs pool the capital of numerous investors.

14. **Risk Tolerance:** An individual investor's ability to accept loss of some or all of the money they have invested.
15. **Robo-Advisor:** A digital platform that provides automated, algorithm-driven financial planning services with little to no human supervision.
16. **Stock:** A type of security that signifies ownership in a corporation and represents a claim on part of the corporation's assets and earnings.
17. **Tax Deduction:** An expense that can be deducted from taxable income. The purpose of tax deductions is to decrease your taxable income, thus reducing your tax liability.

Understanding these terms will equip you with the basic vocabulary needed to comprehend various aspects of financial planning and investment strategies, making it easier to navigate the complex world of personal finance.

Conclusion

As we conclude our journey through the diverse and dynamic world of wealth building for young adults, let's reflect on the key takeaways and reinforce the idea that the path to financial independence is both challenging and rewarding.

Recap of Key Takeaways for Building Wealth as a Young Adult

1. **The Power of Starting Early:** Embrace the magic of compound interest and the significant advantages of starting your investment journey as soon as possible.
2. **Smart Money Management:** Master the basics of budgeting, credit management, and smart spending. Remember, wealth isn't just about how much you earn, but how wisely you manage it.
3. **Diverse Investment Strategies:** From stocks and real estate to alternative investments like collectibles, diversifying your portfolio is key to mitigating risks and capitalizing on different market opportunities.

4. **Leveraging Technology:** Utilize technology, including apps and platforms, to streamline budgeting and investing, and stay informed about emerging opportunities like cryptocurrencies.
5. **Continuous Education:** Always stay curious and eager to learn. The financial world is constantly evolving, and staying informed is crucial for success.
6. **Building Networks:** Engage with mentors, join investment clubs, and participate in financial communities to broaden your knowledge and open doors to new opportunities.

Encouragement for Continued Learning and Growth

The journey to building wealth is not a destination but a continuous path of learning and growth. Embrace every experience as an opportunity to learn — whether it's a success or a setback. Stay adaptable, open to new ideas, and willing to adjust your strategies as the financial landscape changes.

Final Words of Advice for the Journey Ahead

As you move forward on your wealth-building journey, remember to balance ambition with wisdom. Be bold in your pursuits, but cautious in your decisions. Remember, wealth is not just measured in monetary terms, but in the richness of your experiences and the wisdom gained along the way. Maintain a healthy balance between planning for the future and enjoying the present. Finally, never underestimate the impact of small, consistent actions – they are the foundation of great achievements.

Your path to financial freedom is uniquely yours – embrace it with confidence, patience, and a spirit of continuous learning. Here's to a future of abundance, security, and personal fulfillment!

www.ingramcontent.com/pod-product-compliance
Lightning Source LLC
Chambersburg PA
CBHW062250290526
45794CB00006B/2484